GOD'S *Love* UNLIMITED
TO HEALING

Ginger Noyes Antoine

WESTBOW
PRESS®
A DIVISION OF THOMAS NELSON
& ZONDERVAN

Scripture taken from the Holy Bible, NEW INTERNATIONAL
VERSION®. Copyright © 1973, 1978, 1984 by Biblica, Inc. All rights
reserved worldwide. Used by permission. NEW INTERNATIONAL
VERSION® and NIV® are registered trademarks of Biblica, Inc.
Use of either trademark for the offering of goods or services
requires the prior written consent of Biblica US, Inc.

WestBow Press books may be ordered through
booksellers or by contacting:

WestBow Press
A Division of Thomas Nelson & Zondervan
1663 Liberty Drive
Bloomington, IN 47403
www.westbowpress.com
1 (866) 928-1240

Because of the dynamic nature of the Internet, any web addresses or
links contained in this book may have changed since publication and
may no longer be valid. The views expressed in this work are solely those
of the author and do not necessarily reflect the views of the publisher,
and the publisher hereby disclaims any responsibility for them.

Any people depicted in stock imagery provided by Thinkstock are
models, and such images are being used for illustrative purposes only.
Certain stock imagery © Thinkstock.

ISBN: 978-1-5127-3901-5 (sc)

Print information available on the last page.

WestBow Press rev. date: 4/28/2016

Contents

DEDICATED TO GOD

GINGER ANTOINE

Preface

It is in thanksgiving to God for the writings of "God's
Unlimited Love to Healing." This book is to give
Honor to God, a Heart of Generosity for mankind
to be transformed to the Image of God. How great
is God's compassion and kindnesses! I am deeply
in heart, thankful for God's Mercy of insights to
the Spiritual World through the Holy Bible, New
International Version (R)copyright © 1973. Praise
God, as I live each day, the Eternal Light has guided
me through childhood, marriage, brokenness
and to love in the freedom of Righteousness.

It is through many trials, tribulations, and interactions
with soldiers that changed my life. Many tears and Faith
in God has strengthened and shaped my life in such a
miraculous wonder of events. The contents of this book
is composed of understanding: thoughts, emotions, fears,
marriage, restoration, dangers of the mind, the Gospel's
Plan of Salvation, soldier's lives, leaders, examples;
guidelines and evidence of scriptures towards Healing.

How glorious is man's Spirit living within God!
Such is the Joy of knowing that every Soul has the

intelligence and capability to love with the intensity Character of God. May I be humbled in Spirit to share and express that Faith living in every one of us, can overcome all things in life. Thus, uniting our Spirits to God! It is with outpouring love for the many: TBI, PTSD, Suicidal, Depression, Drugs, Alcohol, DUI, Marriage and Divorce, and Deaths.

United We Stand In Victory, towards Healing of the Heart. I thank God for my dear husband, Joseph Antoine, who loves me for what I am and pushes me forward to be what I can be.

<u>GOD BLESS AMERICA AND LOVE TO ALL!</u>

Our thanks go out to everyone. Thank you for being a special part of our lives. We Praise God for you and love you with all our Heart:

- Minister Gary Pollard-(Church of Christ, Fayetteville, NC) Praise be to God for your Unconditional Love and Teachings of Scriptures.
- Minister Paul Mason-(Church of Christ, Fayetteville, NC) Praise be to God, for your outstanding insights of scriptures in challenging many Souls to God.
- Minister Chris Covington-(Church of Christ, Fayetteville, NC) Praise be to God for a Heart like Titus for The Undying Love of Jesus Christ.
- Our Soldiers and Families at Fort Bragg, Fayetteville, N.C.-Praise be to God for your Dedications, Sacrifice, Support, Time, Love, and Patience for America and throughout the World.
- Families, and surrounding communities-Praise be to God for your Love, Support, Patience, Dedications for America, and Base.

The two soldiers in black on the front page, represents a unity of purpose towards Spiritual Freedom of Righteousness, and it is drawn in pen and ink.

Thank you God for guiding my hands. Joseph and I Prayed that through the writings of this book, The Lord will bless many Hearts to the Generosity of God'S Unlimited Healing.

Intro to God's
Unlimited Love to Healing

Psalm 63:1-3:

"O God, you are my God, earnestly I seek you; my soul thirsts for you, my body longs for you, in a dry and weary land where there is no water. I have seen you in the sanctuary and beheld your power and your glory. Because your love is better than life, my lips will glorify you. I will praise you as long as I live, and in your name I will lift up my hands."

God, how great is your Name, for you are a Great King. Heaven and Earth rejoices in the abundance of your Glory. The crops of the fields sing praises to you! Does anyone not enjoy the splendor in nature? All things which you have created, is for your creations.

Mankind is dependent upon the necessities which you have provided. What wonders that you have endowed a man's life with ideas and inventions of new modern technologies towards prosperity. Each living creature so unique in form and temperance. The world is filled with much beauty, wants, desires, temptations and challenges. Each day is an experience, a reality to explore, expand and to conquer the emotions within the Heart.

Emotions and Fears

Emotions are essential to our existence. It is a process that enables us to be transformed to the great purpose of God's Eternal Love. If your emotions are consistently focused and weighed down in negativity, it will spread like cancer throughout the entire Spirit and become a stronghold that is hard to break free. Often times an individual may experience depression, anger, fear, guilt, rejection, withdrawal and accusation, which could lead to explosive destruction to others as well as to one self.

How magnificent it is that one can overcome these corruptive sinful natures! One can be set free to the glorious realm of peace. Pray to God with all your heart!

"Holy Father God I come to you in Spirit and in Truth, for you are a great king, and Great is your name. Everything is possible with you. I asked in my prayers and petitions that you will open my heart and give me understanding, joy, love and peace. May all the Praise, Glory, and Honor be yours, in Jesus name, Amen."

1 Chronicles 28: 9

> *"And you, my son Solomon, acknowledge the God of*
> *your father, and serve him with wholehearted devotion*
> *and with a willing mind, for the Lord searches every*
> *heart and understands every motive behind the*
> *thoughts. If you seek him, he will be found by you;*
> *but if you forsake him, he will reject you forever."*

The human mind is evidently in the hand of God. It is up to man to make a decision to trust completely in God. God is our confidence because God is just and righteous. The communication, prayers and humbleness to God is heard. One must be ready to listen and seek with the understanding of the character of God. All oppositions must be dealt with. For over the course of time, as God is willing, everything is made new. God has the power to refine the spirit within us. The scriptures are given to us because it is spiritual life, which guides our spirit to discern between right and wrong. Our spirit is confident for the power of the word living in us.

1 John 4: 18

> *"There is no fear in love. But perfect love drives*
> *out fear, because fear has to do with punishment.*
> *The one who fears is not made perfect in love."*

Fear can be transformed through dreams, repetitious meditated thinking. Playing with the thoughts of the mind to influence an individual towards negative actions, to control and manipulate certain wants, desires, temptations, and habits. Therefore, one must exercise positive self control, and openness of thought. Each thought must be captured in righteousness quickly and be deleted if it is contrary to the spirit. All negative thoughts are dangerous, for it influences us to take action.

2 Corinthians 10: 5

> *"We demolish arguments and every pretension that sets itself up against the knowledge of God, and we take captive every thought to make it obedient to Christ. And we will be ready to punish every act of disobedience, once your obedience is complete."*

God is the creator of all creations. Our relationship with God should be of obedience, commitment and faith. Nothing can change us when we are one in Christ. By standing firmly in the heart of God (mind, thoughts, and emotions), we are victorious; the flesh may perish, but the spirit lives.

Romans 15: 13

> *"May the God of hope fill you with all joy and peace as you trust in Him, so that you may overflow with hope by the power of the Holy Spirit."*

As God is willing, God's spirit is given to us for his will and purposes. God knows us when we are in our mother's womb. God is compassionate in love for us and can discipline mankind according to our conducts and deeds.

Romans 12: 2

> *"Do not conform any longer to the pattern of this world, but be transformed by the renewing of your mind. Then you will be able to test and approve what God's will is – his good, pleasing and perfect will."*

When we can take the action by surrendering our thoughts, minds and emotions to trust in God completely, we can experience the beauty of God's guidance into the glorious realm of transformation. This is a rare gift that only God can give to us. We must admit our sins and confess it before God, for God is compassionate and is of kindness.

Jeremiah 3: 15

> *"Then I will give you shepherds after my own heart, who will lead you with knowledge and understanding."*

This clearly means that God is faithful in giving guidance through God's chosen spiritual servants.

Jeremiah 3: 22

> *"Return, faithless people; I will cure you of your backsliding." "Yes, we will come to you, for you are the Lord our God."*

One must concentrate solely on God's word and to be strengthened by his power for direction and insight. Consistent faithfulness and willingness will produce a harvest of fruits to overcome the trials and tribulations in life.

A Soldier's Life

Deuteronomy 20: 2- 4

*"When you are about to go into battle, the priest shall
come forward and address the army. He shall say:
"Hear, O Israel: today you are going into battle against
your enemies. Do not be fainthearted or afraid; Do not
be terrified or give way to panic before them. For the
Lord your God is the one who goes with you to fight
for you against your enemies to give you victory."*

Did God not let us understand the events that take place
in a soldier's life? Faith is everything. The Almighty
God strengthens you to endure hardships of discipline
for skills, understanding and knowledge of integrity and
righteousness.

How vigilant is a man trained to protect and overcome
endless days of freezing cold, rain, snow, sleet, and scorching
heat in dusty, windy, and muddy lands. The infested
insects, and wild animals constantly tortured them. With
many days of hunger, and staggering of sleeplessness,
their bodies endured sores and blisters. They had denied

6

themselves of comfort and risked their life to pursue the welfare of others.

O soldiers, the ordeals that you may go through! Many days soaking and freezing in your sticky, smelly, and itchy uniforms that clung to your body. Your belly was hungry and growling for food through endless days of training, and deployment in defending your country. So many days separated from loved ones, created broken relationships, and sleepless nights treading through terrains. Then when you were able to sustain food, your fingers were so cold that you could not even open your MREs!

The boots that you were wearing were sheer torture. Your feet sometimes bled from excessive walking. How much more can you endure? The ruck sack weighed heavy on your tired, sore backs that were shredding every ounce of strength to your destination. At times, a picture of your sweetheart, or family came in your mind. So fleeting joy or sadness took you away for the moment, yet you must still march on.

There came a time when you survived through missions of bloodshed and atrocities. You became broken and battered as a whirlwind of destruction after the storm. Now you are a changed man that will never be as before. Yet if you look on the outside at the whole picture of this new man you have become, God has carried you through the mist of darkness. Soldiers, you have conquered and can run the good race to that glorious hope that God intended for you.

How much more can one be used for the greater glory, Amen! Why? Because you are significantly a spiritual part of God. How can one fight the battle for God, or for anyone without experience, insight, knowledge, and understanding? Many great leaders, apostles, prophets, and judges have to be disciplined as well as worthy to be a servant of God. Most of them are generally ordinary men often with not many skills. Changes is brokenness, yet through the ordeals, the dividing wall is broken down. It is the barrier that has kept one from God.

How Great Are Changes In Life?

Matthew 19: 26

"Jesus looked at them and said, "With man this is impossible, but with God all things are possible."

How magnificent it is for mankind to be blessed in every way so that he could achieve his ultimate goals.

As a young man, you may not know what you want to be in life. So you may decide to enter the military. These are days of tests, trials, and perhaps nervous moments. Yet many days through training and disciplines give you confidence. Then you're able to perform many tasks easily. If you are used to getting your own way, well guess what? You'll be in for a big surprise! Because no matter what jobs or positions you're in, the many comforts are taken from you. Then certainly you will learn to work harder to prove that you are just as intelligent as others.

I remember when I first learned how to cook, my mother made me cook every day! How clumsy I was! Carrying a glass of water, spilling or dropping the glass to the floor! Boiling meat until it's burnt crisp. This training and discipline guided me in days to come. And to top it all off, I thought that I would grow up and become a pretty young lady, but I'm blessed with coke bottle eyeglasses, crooked teeth, and one quarter inch pimples all over my face and body! If you think that you would bloom like a flower, through your puberty years with grace,... well you are certainly no model. Because when you walk you seem to bing and bang, tripping all over things. What a beautiful sight that you have become. Needless to say, everyone put you down and told you that you were not good at anything! Well, you have become a fearful spirit of low self esteem.

I remember as a little girl, I used to run and splash in the rain with other children. It was one of the happiest times to be remembered. The sound of a dog barking happily and raindrops fell upon the joy of glittering faces of the innocents. There were sunny days racing across the open fields and cemetery. Among sounds of cheering, giggling children chasing after the droppings of supplies from the American planes. What a joy to taste a piece of bubble gum. Life was so carefree, seeing through the eyes of a child, roaming throughout the streets of Saigon and deep corners of the villages barefoot with no restrictions or care of dangers.

During the monsoon season it would rain for days flooding throughout the villages. There is nothing like eating a bowl of rice and fish sauce. It sure tasted so good when you're stranded on a straw bed looking at the muddy water closing in on you. Praise God for Grandma, one leg amputated from war, yet struggling to feed her grandchildren! Everyday you had to tread through muddy waters to the open markets for food. There is nothing like the fresh fish, fruits, and vegetables that God provides!

Yet there is a melancholy depression of the heart, experiencing the sight of old men with no legs or arms, dragging themselves throughout the markets begging for help. As a child you think only of what excitement and acceptance that life is! Little feet hopping and sliding through the narrow alleys. Houses side by side, overlooking dark gloomy rivers. The sounds of neighbors chattering and echoing through the stairs and adjoining rooms exposed through cracks, lacking every privacy. The river flows softly among old wooden planks and small openings for latrines. Parts of old broken nets floated here and there. Men fishing along small wooden decks and doorways with the sun beating profusely across their straw hats, to shade as much of their face as they can.

This simple way of life is a purpose of acceptance and humility that is instinctively upheld. War is a terrible thing, yet God has shielded many from the atrocities. So many families got separated, like husbands, wives, children, and friends. The ones that made it to America had the greatest blessing of destiny. So many families were not reunited for many years. Divorces and relationships broken, but also death occurrences. When reunited, you would have to go through much adjustments.

Being a young child, such separation causes uncertainties and distrust when your family is reunited. You don't know how to love like you should. Thank God that as the years progressed, in a loving environment and maturity, you learn how to cope with everyday life. After the fall of Saigon so many escaped through the small fishing boats during the night. Overloading with men, women, and children, empty handed. Such is homelessness crossing the oceans, stifling children from cries in silence. Many days exhausted, packed like sardines, deprived of food and water. Yet longing for compassionate rescuers. So many boats were plundered by pirates, young girls raped, bodies tossed in the ocean, and yet those sinking, their cries haunting the many. Then there are those that had to return to utter consequences. Amer-Asians, children sleeping on streets in homelessness.

Many years have gone by, I thank God for delivering me to a destiny of purpose. I have been disciplined and thankful for God's love.

Oh gracious Holy Father God, that your purpose for the many, that made it to safety. There is no one like you, giving divine mercy of living a life of prosperity. To have become what we are today, are miracles in itself.

Jeremiah 17: 7- 8

> *"But blessed is the man who trusts in the Lord.*
> *Whose confidence is in him. He will be like a tree*
> *planted by the water that sends out its roots by*
> *the stream. It does not fear when heat comes; its*
> *leaves are always green. It has no worries in a*
> *year of drought and never fails to bear fruit."*

Praise God for such changes in a modernized world as today, to exist and appreciate everything that is of God. There is nothing like the guidance of our Holy Father. By careful examination of our life, we will be able to depict the weaknesses and strengths in ourselves.

Taxi days

Have you ever been a taxi cab driver? It is quite an experience! If you are inexperienced, you are in for a rude awakening. It is a job that you can enjoy once you get the swing of things or you might be out of your mind to no end. Do you know how you used to play sports at competitions? Well that's how it is. You're racing towards the finish line for that prize. If you are on the base or off base, you better know the street route, because after 10 to 15 minutes, you are considered slow! It is a job of great patience and love. But most of all, it's faith. The reasons are that you will meet many challenges of personalities, odd hours and unpredictable changes.

There may be days that you do not know where you are at or when you will get home! Sometimes when it would be raining profusely at 2 or 3 o'clock in the morning, and you found yourself out in the country, you better praise God that your husband has given you the flashlight before you left home! Why? Because out in the quiet darkness of the night the wind blows the signs, should you make a right or left? Praise God that you made the correct turn to find the person that you were looking for. Sometimes the person that you look for is not there or they do not respond to a phone call.

Taxi cabbing can take its toll on your health. It requires great endurance, perseverance, strength and compassion. Always, you are deeply in heart sorry to disappoint the customers.

Even if dangers lies ahead, we know that the Lord will bring us home safely in His loving arms. It is in thanksgiving to God for the opportunity to serve our soldiers, family and the surrounding areas. It is such a joy to see the fleeting glow in their faces and perhaps in some small way I could contribute to their cause. It's painful when you cannot be there for them, due to the personal health and circumstances. Everything has its time and seasons. Yet how great is love, for we certainly need each other.

One day I was driving with three officers to the airport, I got a flat tire. I was blessed because they had helped me change my tire within 10 to 15 minutes. Their teamwork was amazing! I will always remember on a hot day, soldiers would even bring me iced tea, a cold water bottle, and tips from the heart. Each day is a day of faith, serving others and thanking God for their thoughtfulness. Let us sing songs to the Lord, for he is pleased!

Hebrews 12: 2

> *"Let us fix our eyes on Jesus, the author and perfecter of our faith, who for the joy set before him endured the cross, scorning its shame, and sat down at the right hand of the throne of God."*

Such glorious compassion and kindness in heart is the Lord. How is it that our Creator allows humanity to be of the utmost consideration? We need to meditate upon this closely, then we can surely identify the many imperfections that we make in life.

What Great Leadership Is

2 Samuel 19: 6- 8

"You love those who hate you and hate those who love you. You have made it clear today that the commanders and their men mean nothing to you. I see that you would be pleased if Absalom were alive today and all of us were dead. Now go out and encourage your men. I swear by the Lord that if you don't go out, not a man will be left with you by nightfall. This will be worse for you than all the calamities that have come upon you from your youth till now. So the King got up and took his seat in the Gateway. When the men were told, "The king is sitting in the Gateway," they all came before him."

Pain, griefs, troubles, humiliation and challenges shall come. It is a discipline and testing of the conscience. Yet absolutely there is ultimate joy that triumphs in victory throughout the miraculous power of God. Praise be to God, that one can deny oneself comfort, the pureness of heart to give to the needs of others is much greater. The Lord has shown us through one of the most tumultuous point in King David's life. King David was faced with a horrific intensity, execution death of his son, Absalom; threatened of his position and moral, righteousness of the kingdom. So great is the heart, when it is broken into so many pieces. The choices that we make maybe productive, or it can result in catastrophic consequences.

Jeremiah 17: 9

> *"The heart is deceitful above all things and beyond cure. Who can understand it?"*

It is in thanksgiving to God for His everlasting patience towards mankind. How much so in life, that man had challenge against the living God? God's teachings, disciplines and examples greatly is a love that foresees, surpasses all troubles. Yet refining mankind to the ultimate blessings of God's glorious generosity.

David was a man who understood God, as a very young man; already the Lord had trained him into keeping his father's sheep. The consistency of fighting off lions, bears and other wild animals, strengthen him in so many areas. In order to achieve goals, success, and military warfare tactics, one must be challenged to obtain self control, perseverance, organization skills, character and importantly faith. Without faith, how can one serve God and to protect countrymen, families with purpose of integrity and justice?

Psalm 22: 10

> *"From birth I was cast upon you; from my mother's womb you have been my God."*

Spiritually, David was already clearly of close relationship with God.

2 Samuel 11: 2

"One evening, David got up from his bed and walked around on the roof of the palace. From the roof he saw a woman bathing. The woman was very beautiful, and David sent someone to find out about her. The man said, "isn't this Bathsheba, the daughter of Eliam, and the wife of Uriah the Hittite?"

How utterly tragic is the introduction of thoughts, for it works on the emotions. We must be extremely careful at all times. God gives us such an example to understand that the human mind alone is so vulnerable to fall if it is not molded and grounded in love. The lust of the eyes is extremely deadly. Our heart and the innermost spiritual aspect of us must be centered on God. There must be the consistency of deep love and respect--- a total commitment of agreement. Training and disciplines require much perseverance because the world that we are facing is of operative evil desires.

John 8: 7

"When they kept on questioning him, he straightened up and said to them, "If any one of you is without sin, let him be the first to throw a stone at her."

This passage pertains to the woman caught in adultery. So much is to be learned here. How merciful is the love of God. When God speaks, mankind listens in silence, for God's Word is authoritative, upright and just. God teaches us to examine ourselves closely, to know in our heart that everyone of us sin. Therefore, by recognizing our inadequacy and downfalls, we can begin to love and have compassion for others. We can certainly forgive others for the offenses. At times the offense may seem unbearable, but with much patience, sincere faith, prayers and petitions to God would be answered. Because God is faithful in every way to break down all strongholds towards peace. The mind must be sifted, purified and humbled before the living God. So many great leaders have had much experiences and brokenness, so that they can be used for much greater things in life.

1 Samuel 16: 7

"But the Lord said to Samuel, "Do not consider his appearance or his height, for I have rejected him. The Lord does not look at the things man looks at. Man looks at the outward appearance, but the Lord looks at the heart."

How merciful and glorious is God, to bless mankind with the spiritual insight! Each and everyone of us is significantly and uniquely created for God's purpose. God has shown us through David, that the heart is so important to God; for it is the central thought of our thinking. Individually, each being is a special part of God. God had allowed David to see the imperfections in himself, experience consequences, the brokenness of such extent; thus, becoming Israel's king.

Great sufferings are an endurance that can become gloriously Godly sorrows, which magnificently enables the Spirit in us to be of sincere contriteness. A heart that is deeply sorry, will be able to Love and forgive with much humbleness and meekness. Through many troubles and events taken place in David's life, great teachings for mankind to be knowledgeable is evident. It is God's generosity of heart to let the souls understand that we are One Spirit. David was after God's heart. One can overcome all things through the Eternal love of God. It is absolutely possible because love must be trained and tested in every way.

A heart that is truly compassionate, will not look down on others at merely glances, opinions, or gossip but it is soul deep searching of meekness, mercy and the fearful wrath of God. All the tears that one sheds can never be enough like the unconditional love of God. It is Thanksgiving to God for opening the mind to understand that circumstances are a process to become what we are today. All things of the past has taught us to appreciate and value a more meaningful purpose to the Glory of God. A beauty, exceedingly filled with the pureness Light of God.

Psalms 106:3

"Blessed are they who maintain justice,
who constantly do what is right."

The Lord gives us his peace to overcome the shadows of our life to His Glorious Light. All negative can turn to positive. One cannot allow Satan to control his thoughts and imprisonment of the Eternal Destruction. How can one give up his Soul to such deadly influence of the mind? Should one destroy everything that one worked so hard for. Humanity is not perfect. Righteousness is completely a way to Joy, Love and Peace.

The imperfections in life is a great lesson to be learned. It is a process to mature and ripen to Eternal Spiritual Fruits of the Children of God. The children of tomorrow needs us. Though our pain may be excruciating, it is nothing as close as the suffering of Jesus at the cross. We are strong and courageous because the power of God is living in us. We are planted in the root of the branch to lead the many Souls to God.

Genesis 45:7

> *"But God sent me ahead of you to preserve*
> *for you a remnant on earth and to save*
> *your lives by a great deliverance."*

How marvelous is it to be blessed with God's words! The story of Joseph shows us a great destiny of purpose. Joseph who tends flocks, was sold into slavery by his brothers out of jealousy and the interpretations of his dreams. But because the Lord was with him, he was able to save the people from famine through many complexities, chained shackled imprisonment journey in life.

How can a man become a great leader as well as the protector for his country and family?

Hebrews 12: 11

"No discipline seems pleasant at the time, but painful. Later on, however, it produces a harvest of righteousness and peace for those who have been trained by it."

Romans 5: 3-5

"Not only so, but we also rejoice in our sufferings, because we know that suffering produces perseverance: perseverance, character; and character, hope. And hope does not disappoint us, because God has poured out his love into our hearts by the Holy Spirit, whom he has given us."

It is in Thanksgiving to God for everything that God created. There is a purpose. In life, one does not know what will be. The events and occurrences will change us to make a decision. God had given us his unconditional love to conquer our physical self to the regenerated Spirit of God. We must have the experiences so that we can relate to others, to share and thus, making a difference and unity to become One.

Matthew 10: 28

> *"Do not be afraid of those who kill the body but*
> *cannot kill the soul. Rather, be afraid of the One*
> *who can destroy both soul and body in hell."*

The reality of life and the choices that we make can either be painful or rewarding. Even though tragic are the circumstances in life, there is an absolute way to freedom! All the fears, flashbacks or unworthiness can be set free because we are the image of God. Confidence and Trust is explicitly shown to all truth in scriptures. What joy it is that the Lord has given us a love of such purity, spiritual transformation to Eternity. Let the Spirit within us unite to God in complete unity. For love conquers all.

How Compassionate is The Lord?

Far deep in the country, a boyish little girl grew up, tagging along beside grandma everywhere she went. There is nothing as beautiful as the blue skies, open meadows, flowing streams and rivers! So many days catching fish and crabs, making nets, gathered fruits and raised chickens. Those were the happiest days to be remembered till grandma passed away. Living with mama and her brother was a total living nightmare! Papa had passed away when she was just three. Then grandma passed away, life was upside down. Mama had such a troubled past, that so many days she was so full of unimaginable anger. So many days weeks, months, and years of beatings from mom and her brother. There was a time that her hair was snatched tight, repeated slaps went on and on... The bruises filled her little form, marks and welts across her flesh.

She often wondered who is God and why did God allow this to be so. Often she would climb to hide, so fearful that she would get beaten again. No matter where she was, she was found and brought back for another beating! By the time she was 14 she was forced to marry. If she had thought that this would change, matters only got worse when her husband was just as abusive as her mother. And as she matured over the next few years, recognizing that if she continued to stay, her children and her life would be a total disaster.

The shame and humiliation of suffering has scarred her so greatly that she was afraid to share every detail with anyone. One day she found courage through neighbors and friends. She escaped with her children to the cities. Whatever it took sweeping floors, or waitressing, she would work to provide for her children. Life was tough, yet through the tears and sorrows what joy is freedom! She learned to live again and can share her experiences to others, **What A Price Is Freedom**. As time went by, she met a soldier, who was unloved and forgotten among siblings. Their love grew for each other rapidly. She would cut his steak in tiny little pieces that no one ever cared to do. And he loved her children as his own.

Today 50 years later, **The Lord Is Good!** Tears of joy because through it all it is such a blessing to see the strength, character, and accomplishments that the children and grandchildren have become.

1 John 4: 12

> *"No one has ever seen God; but if we love one another,*
> *God lives in us and his love is made complete in us."*

It's difficult to love those who have caused us so much pain and grief. There is no one like God. The love of God is embedded deeply in our heart. The harsh reality in life, taught us how to love one another. Why? Because we all need love. Love does no evil, for it overlooks the imperfections and gives unconditionally. When Love has reached the ultimate point, it is seeing through the spiritual eyes of God to forgive!

Understanding the Gospel Plan of Salvation

Understanding the gospel plan of salvation is significantly rewarding in seeking God for understanding and knowledge. God is perfection. Everything God created is perfect in form, texture, color and purpose. God has provided everything for us to enjoy, and utilizes the abilities to think and to reason. Praise God for the unlimited love, before the world began.

1 Corinthians 15: 3

> *"For what I received I passed on to you as of first importance: That Christ died for our sins according to the Scriptures, that he was buried, that he was raised on the third day according to the Scriptures, and that he appeared to Peter, and then to the Twelve."*

We must come to God with a sincere heart, willingness to receive the gospel plan of salvation. God himself, has shown us his ultimate outpouring love by laying down his life for us at the cross.

The Gospel's Plan Of Salvation:

Hear	Romans 10:17, Acts 2: 17
Believe	Acts 19: 18, John 3: 14 - 17
Repent	John 16: 13, Luke 13: 3, Act 17: 30
Confess	Luke 12: 8, Romans 10: 9, Matthew 10: 32
Baptized	Matthew 3: 13 - 17, Colossians 2: 12, Act 2: 38
Faithful	1 Corinthians 1: 9, Revelations 2: 10, Deuteronomy 7: 9

Ephesians 2: 15-18

> *"By abolishing in his flesh the law with its commandments and regulations. His purpose was to create in himself one new man out of the two, thus making peace, and in this one body to reconcile both of them to God through the cross, by which he put to death their hostility. He came to preach to you who were far away and peace to those who are near. For through him we both have access to the Father by one Spirit."*

God had destroyed the power of death. We have the confidence of knowing God's unconditional gift to eternal life. We have the protection of guidance through baptism, which the Holy Spirit can work in us to all Truths.

John 16: 15

> *"All that belongs to the Father is mine. That is why I said the Spirit will take from what is mine and make it known to you."*

God's genuine unconditional love is like no other. Our one and only Holy Father has reached out to us through endless tears and the shedding blood of his beloved son Jesus. Jesus completely shared all that is within him, spiritual blessings to children of God!

Hebrews 2: 14-18

"Since the children have flesh and blood, he too shared in the humanity so that by his death he might destroy him who holds the power of death - that is the devil - and free those who all their lives were held in slavery by their fear of death. For surely it is not angels he helps, but Abraham's descendants. For this reason he had to be made like his brothers in every way, in order and that he might become a merciful and faithful high priest in service to God, and that he might make atonement for the sins of the people. Because he himself suffered when he was tempted, he is able to help those who are being tempted."

The Way to A Successful Marriage and Restoration

1 Corinthians 7: 5

"Do not deprive each other except by mutual consent and for a time, so that you may devote yourselves to prayer. Then come together again so that Satan will not tempt you because of your lack of self-control."

God has provided humanity the insight of his love to escape the temptation in the world; For the world can rob us of joy and comfort. So many events and tragedies will disable our soul. Therefore, we must pray consistently and consider one another with deep love, respect, communication and agreement. In having a successful relationship, one should consider these many important points:

1. Do you listen and have an open communication?
2. Is there consideration when your significant other is sick and tired?
3. Do you give of yourself and show it in your actions?
4. Do you care and do your best to protect and guide each other?
5. Do you show each other that you are special just the way that God created you?

6. Do you push each other forward to be the best that you can be?
7. Do you sit down with your children to remember God by sharing God's decrees?
8. Though there are differences and interests, do you try to make things more enjoyable so that it will bring you closer together?
9. Jobs and children may distract you, do you make time to refresh your love so that it can bloom with each passing day?
10. Do you take initiative to get things done as a team?

Jonah 4:10-11

"But the Lord said, "You have been concerned about this vine, though you did not tend it or make it grow. It sprang up overnight and died overnight. But Nineveh has more than a hundred and twenty thousand people who cannot tell their right hand from their left; and many cattle as well. Should I not be concerned about that great city?"

To give in life is consideration. No matter what we experience and deal with, God is there to support us and strengthen us. By contributing our time and energy, physically and mentally to others, the results will be fruitful, productive and healing our wounds as well as our comrades. God has let it be known of his great compassion for humanity through Jonah. It is the teaching to love and to care for everything that is in our life. The constant application and consideration will certainly help us to be productive and effective in our lives.

Genesis 2: 18

*"The Lord God said, "It is not good for the man to
be alone. I will make a helper suitable for him."*

The women in your life is the most beautiful Lily of the
fields. She was created uniquely in every way to unite to
her husband. Will you cherish her in days to come? What
is the beauty you see through her eyes? Years come and
seasons go, will you consider each other like God created
his creations? A heart that is nurtured will always shine
gloriously in harmony like the sun. How precious is the
works of God that created children in His image!

Even though evil comes through introductions of thoughts;
trust not the world, but focus on the integrity and
faithfulness of God. Do not give up on your children! They
may rebuke you to no end, yet always be patient as the
Lord, show you children and let them know that they are
angels of God. Love them tenderly near and far. Always
be proud of them, let them see through your words and
actions. Children are born with such intelligence. All of us
have been blessed with the Divine Power from God.

Time will heal all wounds. The Lord is watching, patiently
and lovingly. There is nothing as magnificent as the
gracious mercy of his miracles. Trust in God, serve him
wholeheartedly. For great is his mercy in sending the spirit
and making all things new. Everything will be refined to
its order. Love is complete because God has considered all
things before the world began.

Proverbs 31: 10- 12

"A wife of noble character who can find? She is worth far more than rubies, her husband has full confidence in her and lacks nothing of value. She brings him good not harm, all the days of her life."

A wife is like a little bird that you held in the palm of your hand. Love her tenderly each passing day, nurture and care for her ever so. How glorious is it when two souls are joined. Maybe she is a little ugly duckling; seek deeply into her inner beauty, then gracefully she will bloom each day like the morning sunrise. Never for a moment take her for granted. Protect her always in integrity and prayers.

Grass grows tall and flowers grow, yet diligently, she cuts and prunes. Making soups and custard pie. Let her not be toiled so, ever so alone but always toiled in harmony. Side by side, together holding hands. In sickness, trials and seasons come; yet a wife will comfort her husband in her loving arms. Many days has come to pass, aging gray so ever so. No more teeth to fill your smile, nevertheless her gentle hands pampered you with hot - steamy oatmeal. Tired eyes, lovingly locked in unity. Sing songs and praise the Lord, for the Lord is pleased and blesses you with each passing day.

The union of two people is so very precious to God.

Ephesians 5: 25 - 27

"Husbands, love your wives, just as Christ loved the church gave himself up for her to make her Holy, cleansing her by the washing with water through the word, and to present her to himself as a radiant church without stain or wrinkle or any other blemish, but holy and blameless."

There is no greater love than the love of Jesus for the church. It is the consuming love for all of his creations. The gospel of Jesus Christ is fulfilled in every way to bring the soul to its ultimate purity and maturity, to honor, praise and to glorify God. There is no one like our the Lord Jesus, who had suffered all things for us. How is it that our One and only Jesus allowed himself to such humbled, lowliness state of the physical for us? For God himself could easily destroy us at any moment without us knowing it! What joy and honor it is to know the consuming glory of God's love! God had prepared everything before the world began. God wants us to be like him in every way. How great is the endless generosity of heart.

Mankind is exquisitely created in every way of such everlasting beauty. A beauty that is within God's Eternal Light. We are One because of the power living in us. It is the blending of the mind, thoughts and emotions. How absolutely glorious to unite in conformity! If we truly love something, we must protect it in every possible way. It is the unconditional love, respect and forgiveness. The conclusion is exceptionally gratifying. There is no need for anything else, because love is complete.

The more that one seeks God wholeheartedly, God showers him with immeasurable insight. The mind opens to spiritual life, like the budding of a flower grasping for rain and sunlight. It blooms in radiant colors. When wisdom comes, how greatly are tears flowing in meekness. God is the greatest builder of all things. God's mighty hands reach out to embrace all life forms to God's eternal glory. The physical of the flesh is so much ever so, because natural self - the body represents a unity of purpose. Therefore, how great is love expressing in marriage. The oneness of heart joining in action, and holiness. A heart that is committed totally in spirit, soul and body, cannot be broken. It is the complete surrendering of self to God.

Restoration

John 16: 33

"I have told you these things, so that in me, you may have peace. In this world you will have trouble. But take heart! I have overcome the world."

Jesus is explicit in his words. Every creation should have this confidence and knowledge. There is no greater love than the love of God. God is the greatest physician and healer. We absolutely must confess our sins before God to be healed. Our Father is the only One that can help us recognize our iniquities and changing us to understand the consuming compassionate love to forgive others for their offenses.

Though we may be dying inside emotionally, God gives us that perfect love to overcome the tears, sorrows and to put love into action. Be not afraid of what the world sees or condemns you for your imperfection; for God understands your pain like no other. Even though as we walk in this world, people who know us for what we have done; Some may ridicule, humiliate or degrade us, we must stand firm and focus solely on God. God's Word gives us strength where no one can hurt us.

Galatians 5: 22

*"But the fruit of the Spirit is love, joy, peace, patience, kindness, goodness, faithfulness, gentleness and self-control. **Against such things there is no law.**"*

Humanity must examine the scripture closely and put it into action! Test God by applying the Fruit of the Spirit in your life. You will certainly see the results of God's power working! This passage is the miraculous spiritual life of mysterious insight to understand the character of God, and to walk in justice and righteousness towards freedom.

Matthew 19:11-12

"Jesus replied, "Not everyone can accept this word, but only those to whom it has been given. For some are eunuchs because they were born that way; others were made that way by men, and others have renounced marriage because of the kingdom of heaven. The one that can accept this should accept it."

Because God is Holy we too must be holy. No matter how painful, a sacrifice and dedication to God should be in faithfulness and holiness in action.

Isaiah 56: 4-5

"For this is what the Lord says: "To the eunuchs who keep my Sabbaths, who choose what pleases me and hold fast to my covenant -- to them I will give within my temple and its walls a memorial and a name better than sons and daughters; I will give them an everlasting name that will not be cut off."

How merciful is God's love! God has shown us by revealing to us his thoughts and examples to follow. It is a promise, a faithfulness that God is true to his word.

Deuteronomy 8: 2-5

"Remember how the Lord your God led you all the way in the desert these forty years, to humble you and to test you in order to know what was in your heart, whether or not you would keep his command. He humbled you, causing you to hunger and then feeding you with manna, which neither you nor your fathers have known. To teach you that man does not live on bread alone but on every word that comes from the mouth of the Lord. Your clothes did not wear out and your feet did not swell during these forty years."

No then in your heart, that as a man disciplines his son, so the Lord your God disciplines you.

The Lord is so patient in his love for us. Each day watching and waiting for his creations to be transformed into the One image of God himself.

John 4: 34

> *"My food," said Jesus, "is to do the will of him*
> *who sent me and to finish his work."*

Jesus paid the full price for our sins, therefore sufferings must be endured and overcome in Confessions of repentance. We cannot allow Satan to destroy us with accusations of a guilty conscience, or self pity, which could lead to negative habits, suicide, and deaths. Today, we live in a society of much divorces and criticism as well as divisions of the churches, establishments, and religions. Our hearts must unite in faith and acknowledgment of God. By surrendering our Spirit to God, then the Holy Spirit can begin to work in us.

John 16:13

> *"But when he, the Spirit of the truth, comes,*
> *he will guide you into all truth."*

The experiences and situations in life can either break us down physically or mentally. Yet God is always there to guide us spiritually. When we have reached the humbleness point, then we start to reconsider each step of action to better our life as well as others. God has opened our heart - that is the mind, thoughts and emotions to understand our errors. The objective is love and forgiveness. The transformation has begun. We can face the world and say please forgive me, I love you no matter what you do to me. This is deep sincerity, contrite in heart and humbleness towards God.

Restoration of the Soul

Confession:

1 John 1: 9

> *"If we confess our sins, he is faithful and
> just and will forgive us our sins and purify
> us from all unrighteousness."*

Luke 12: 8

> *"I tell you whoever acknowledges me before
> men, the Son of Man will also acknowledge
> him before the angels of God."*

Repentance:

Act 17: 30

> *"In the past God overlooked such ignorance, but now
> he commands all people everywhere to repent."*

Trust:

Job 22: 21

> *"Submit to God and be at peace with him; in*
> *this way prosperity will come to you."*

Jeremiah 17: 7 - 8

> *"But blessed is the man who trusts in the Lord, whose*
> *confidence is in him. He will be like a tree planted by*
> *the water that sends out its roots by the stream."*

Contrite:

2 Corinthians 7: 10

> *"Godly sorrow brings repentance that leads to salvation*
> *and leaves no regret, but worldly sorrow brings death."*

Humbleness:

Isaiah 66: 2

> *"Has not my hand made all these things, and*
> *so they came into being?," declares the Lord.*
> *This is the one I esteem: he who is humble and*
> *contrite in spirit and trembles at my word."*

Baptismal:

John 3: 3

> *"In reply, Jesus declared, "I tell you the truth, no one can see the kingdom of God, unless he is born again."*

Holy Spirit:

John 16: 13

> *"But when he, the Spirit of Truth comes, he will guide you into all truth. He will not speak on his own, he will speak only what he hears and he will tell you what is yet to come."*

Jesus:

John 14: 6

> *"Jesus answered, "I am the way and the truth and the life. No one comes to the Father except through me."*

God:

Jeremiah 10: 10

> *"But the Lord is the true God; He is the living God, the eternal king. When he is angry, the earth trembles; the nation's cannot endure his wrath."*

How to be Healed with God's Mercy and Overcome The Battlefield of the Mind

Psalms 116: 1-2

"I love the Lord, for he heard my voice; He heard my cry for mercy, because he turned his ear to me, I will call on the Lord as long as I live.

Each day is a day to be healed. Look at the rising of the Sun in the morning as well as the Sun going down in the afternoon. Everything is in motion.

Matthew 18: 10

"See that you do not look down on one of these little ones. For I tell you that their angels in heaven always see the face of my Father in heaven."

The many impacts and aftermath of the storms open our hearts to lead others towards Heaven's light. We who are strong, will show the weak to love. Is not a child when he is born, not so love already? A life that is nurtured of righteousness will confidently be productive and effective. Unrighteousness is a dissatisfaction of character in fear. When we can forgive and live without fear, it is understanding how to deny oneself for others.

Merciful God

The atrocities of war are damaging in so many ways. Separations, broken homes, relationships, death, and suffering takes a toll. The mind is a battlefield! The consuming introductions thoughts play heavily on the mind and emotions.

Mark 14: 38

"Watch and pray so that you will not fall into temptation. The Spirit is willing, but the body is weak."

Because our bodies are flesh, we must go to the Lord in prayers and petitions. The physical self cannot stand against the forces of darkness. Jesus has conquered and paid the full price for our sins. The Son of God came in the physical form, to be in every way like us, so that we would be guided from the corruptions of the world. The evil world introduce its own thoughts to manipulate and influence us. God gives us the will to choose. A heart that loves unconditionally, will triumph in victory, thus becoming one with the Spirit of God!

Genesis 3: 13

> *"Then the Lord God said to the woman, "What*
> *is this you have done?" The woman said,*
> *"The serpent deceived me, and I ate."*

One must always be alert to the intimidation of others. For it will challenge in every way, using persuasive words, ideas contradicting justice. Turning against what is good. It is potentially destructive, by giving the deceptive emotions to the point of power and control. As we can see here with the falling of mankind through Eve. How quickly is the human mind so quick to change and take action. Do we not have needs and desires as an infant in our mother's womb?

The spirit in us is exceptionally composed of intellectual abilities. Every one of us is so gifted by God. Yet many are unaware of this till there is a change taking place. It is a gradual process in time and place. Knowledge and understanding is obtained through the consistent working of the mind. The Lord has already blessed us abundantly before the world began.

Proverbs 8: 13 - 14

> *"To fear the Lord is to hate evil; I hate pride and arrogance,*
> *evil behavior and perverse speech. Council and sound*
> *judgment are mine; I have understanding and power."*

So can we not love our God? God has shown us a love that surpasses all things. There is no comparison to God. God has ensured the path to the tree of life. What more could we possibly want? The life without God is a life without meaning.

Luke 22: 31 - 32

> *"Simon, Simon, Satan has asked to sift you as wheat. But I have prayed for you, Simon, that your faith may not fail. And when you have turned back, strengthen your brothers."*

In this passage, the Lord is speaking to Peter (Simon). Because Peter would later deny Jesus 3 times. Jesus had let it be known, the great compassion for Peter. Peter was one of the chosen, to do so much more for the gospel. Training and discipline has to be mastered. And every job or position, one has to know its functions, concepts, purposes, and values. The teachings and commitments to God are so much more. By bringing souls to God is no easy task.

2 Corinthians 6:4-10

> *"Rather as servants of God we commend ourselves in every way; in great endurance: in troubles, hardships and distresses; In beatings, imprisonments and riots: in hard work, sleepless nights and hunger; in purity, understanding, patience and kindness; In the Holy Spirit and sincere love; In truthful speech and in the power of God; with weapons of righteousness in the right hand and in the left; through glory and dishonor,*

bad report and good report, genuine, yet regarded as impostors; Known, yet regarded as unknown; dying and yet we live on; beaten, and yet and not killed. Sorrowful, yet always rejoicing, poor yet making many rich; having nothing, and yet possessing everything."

According to the scripture, spoken by the Apostle Paul's hardships to the Corinthians, what tremendous dedications of brokenness, yet racing toward the kingdom of God in power and glory. How significant is the heart of contriteness repenting to the miraculous wonders of God's grace. There is so much more to be learned! God knew how wicked the evil world is, and so God made every preparation for the purpose to come. God has known of man's weaknesses. The spiritual mind of man needed to be strengthened. Faith has always been in us. All that we have to do first is believe.

Romans 2: 9- 11

"There will be trouble and distress for every human being who does evil; First for the Jew, then for the Gentile; but glory, honor and peace for everyone who does good; First for the Jew and then for the Gentile. For God does not show favoritism."

Tis sad the circumstances of life, and God knew of our imperfections. God has given us every knowledge, understanding, and direction to righteousness. We must strengthen one another. There may be times that we may feel so alone, the Lord's presence is always there. That is faith already! Our fear of God is acknowledged when we read God's Word. For God is precise in everything that he does.

Hebrews 4:12

> *"For the Word of God is alive and active."*

We can change from the downfalls of our life to a crowning glory of God.

Romans 9: 18

> *"Therefore God has mercy on whom he wants to have mercy, and he hardens whom he wants to harden."*

How can one understand God so? It requires a deep, zealous attitude towards God. Nothing should stand in our way! When we are faced with much pain in our lives, the spiritual aspect of God is there for us. If we attended church, our main objective is God. If we love with the intensity of God, no one can change it. Because when our pain is so great, the discipline of the Holy Spirit makes us complete as a child seeing the face of God.

Focusing On God

No matter what background you're from, ethnics, or religion, what is most important are the Scriptures foretold. Each person must focus in the heart of God, then all things will fall in order as God will it. It is simply studying and meditating on God's Word. By the consistent devotion to God, one will increase with the abundance of spiritual growth and insight to the enlightenment of God. Mankind is susceptible to errors, suffering, shame, humiliation, deprivation, and brokenness in life. These elements cannot be avoided, for discipline produces understanding of heart.

Jeremiah 17: 10

"I the Lord search the heart and examine the mind, to reward a man according to his conduct, according to what his deeds deserve."

God's words are like no other. It consumes us spiritually, in soul and body. Can one not see how clear, firm and sure it is? If God did not set up boundaries and discipline, will mankind respect him for who he is? By trusting in

God, one knows that the father understands his every thought, worries and needs, for the Mercy is great through the suffering of Jesus. The creations can be transformed in his eternal love.

Spiritual Enlightenment to the Acknowledgment of God

Jeremiah 9: 1

> *"Oh that my head were spring of water and*
> *my eyes a fountain of tears! I would weep day*
> *and night for the slain of my people."*

Our Majesty who is omnipotent, omnipresent, and omniscient (absolute power, present everywhere, knowing everything); has given us the freedom to righteousness. God allowed us to know the endless tears for us to be united with him and share in His glory. Everything that was created, was in accordance to the law of order for the creations. God has denied his very self to ensure that the suffering of Jesus at the cross is to bring us into unity. The Lord Almighty is exceedingly glorious of eternal righteousness and abounding in love.

Generations, and nations upon nations. Let us recognize the magnificent splendor and depth of God's love. The outpouring endless sufferings of those who were predestined for the purpose of the gospel. Remember the destructive desolation throughout the streets of Jerusalem, the towns of Judah from the invasion of peoples of the north, the Babylonians?

Scriptures To Spiritual Enlightenment To The Knowledge Of God:

Jeremiah 25: 9

> *"I will summon all the peoples of the north and my servant Nebuchadnezzar king of Babylon," declares the Lord "and I will bring them against this land and its inhabitants and against all the surrounding nations."*

Jeremiah 25: 18

> *"Jerusalem and the towns of Judah, it's kings and officials to make them a ruin and an object of horror and scorn, a curse, as they are today; v19-v26.*

Jeremiah 9: 7

> *"Therefore this is what the Lord Almighty says: "See, I will refine and test them, for what else can I do because of the sin of my people?"*

2 Kings 17: 13

> *"The Lord warned Israel and Judah through all his prophets and Seers: "Turn from your evil ways. Observe my commands and decrees, in accordance with the entire*

*law that I commanded your fathers to obey and that I
delivered to you through my servants the prophets."*

1 King 11: 35

*"I will take the kingdom from his son's hands and give
you ten tribes. I will give one tribe to his son so that
David my servant may always have a lamp before me
in Jerusalem, the city where I chose to put my name."*

1 King 12: 19

*"So Israel has been in rebellion against
the house of David to this day."*

2 Chronicles 11:4

*"This is what the Lord says: "Do not go up to fight
against your brothers. Go home, everyone of you, for
this is my doing." So they obeyed the words of the Lord
and turned back from marching against Jeroboam."*

2 King 17: 40-41

*"They would not listen, however, but persisted
in their former practices. Even though all these
people were worshiping the Lord, they were
serving their idols. To this day their children and
grandchildren continue to do as their fathers did."*

So much has been written throughout Scriptures for mankind to be knowledgeable in every way about God. But it isn't only about God, for as the seeking of the inner self, certainly there is an explosion of reality, a love that has united mankind from the beginning of time. This was the time that man was one with God, created every way in his likeness. How is it that the inner self got so divided? Is it not of our own choice?

Ezekiel 28: 14

> *"You are anointed as a guardian*
> *cherub, for so I ordained you."*

How much more so in this passage that the ultimate love of God is shown.

Ezekiel 28: 17

> *"Your heart became proud on account of your*
> *beauty, and you corrupted your wisdom because*
> *of your splendor. So I threw you to the earth,*
> *I made a spectacle of you before kings."*

Hallelujah! When love expresses through such extent of generosity. How faithful that there should be a unity of praise, of glory and honor. But tragically is a changing heart. Now the question is this, can one count how many teardrops fall from the eyes of God? The beloved Son of God, Jesus, dripping ever so in blood, all the way to Golgotha; enduring all evil corruptions for mankind at the cross.

John 17: 24

> *"Father, I want those you have given me to be*
> *with me where I am and to see my glory, the*
> *glory you have given me because you have*
> *loved me before the creation of the world.'*

Where there is love, there is great joy. How many more infants be born to suffer the endless Wars? God has reached out to mankind through the greatest spiritual of self denying. Jesus the beloved Son of God as the sacrificial lamb; through him, all souls are confidently filled with the inheritance of God. How often it is to experience the 9 months of pregnancy both mother and father experience the emotional changes. What joy is the breathing of an infant, and to see the years of puberty and maturity. No matter how harsh the reality of life that we find ourselves in, the love that we have for our children pierces us internally.

Our heart goes out to them in every way of teaching, but importantly to be respected with the willingness of dignity. Some of us are fortunate to grow up in a stable environment, and some may have to struggle through the brokenness of homes, wars, and differences in cultures and religions. The mind is composed of good and evil. Oneself must be disciplined with perseverance. Mankind is so much more than he can imagine. This self in us is of exceptional attributes of God. It is the decision, making part of us.

Genesis 2: 7

*"The Lord God formed the man from the dust of the
ground and breathed into his nostrils the breath
of life, and the man became a living being."*

How glorious it is to be that significant part of God. Our
Creator knows of our every existence and personalities.
Each and everyone of us is spiritually gifted. Scattered
throughout the world. Yet miraculously, we share the one
and only Holy Father, God. In any impact there are grief
and changes taking place. The outer shell of us is broken,
to be replaced and strength of character. The inner spirit
of us can triumph with the glorious workings of the Holy
Spirit, truth of faith.

There was a young man, working as a gas attendant. He
had an uncontrollable energy and zest in life. The boss
gave him multitasks from registers to gas pump, stocking
to deliveries. Then changing tires of every kind, whether it
was family trucks, Motor cycles, bicycles, and cars – 4, 6,
and 8 cylinders. He had to master them all. At times even
tractor tires. Praise the Lord, there's chisel and sledge
hammers to pry them apart.

Now comes a time down in Jamaica Queens, working
alongside with coworkers, that the thief came. Pointing the
gun at the attendant saying open the door and give me all
the cash! The attendant answered "Why don't you go down
the street and rob the other guy!" Surprisingly the robber
left in discontent. A few days later the attendant was alone

working, came the same robber. "Fool!" He said, pointing the gun at him, "you think I'm joking this time, give me the cash." The attendant gave him the cash. And the robber knocked everything over.

Telephone lines jerked off the hook. Glory be to God that the attendant is not hurt, for it was told that the last attendant was shot dead from a robbery. Nevertheless, this young man continued on with his life. Even when days of sleeping on trains, selling newspapers at $0.25, cold wintery dampness and broken relationships cannot destroy him. Because faith living in him so richly, not looking back at the past, but to push forward in victory. Over the years the Lord had been so good to him, for changing the lives of people to be successful.

Philippians 3: 13 - 14

"Brothers, I do not consider myself yet to have taken hold of it. The one thing I do: forgetting what is behind and straining toward what is ahead. I press on toward the goal to win the prize for which God has called me heavenward in Christ Jesus."

Every soul is precious in the sight of God. By looking in the mirror we see ourselves. So as the years pass by, what do we see looking back at us today? There is so much for us to be accomplished. The childish outer self fades, yet an illuminated glowing inner self is exploding in rays of spectrums towards heaven. The spirit lives on. Truth guide us through all things.

Revelation 4: 11

*"You are worthy, our Lord and God, to receive glory
and honor and power, for you created all things and
by your will they were created and have their being."*

Holy Father God, your words living in us ever so. You knew us before we were in our mother's wombs. Though we are scattered throughout the world, your love is evident. Your eyes see all that is in the world.

Ezekial 24: 14

*"I the LORD have spoken. The time has come for me
to act. I will not hold back; I will not have pity, nor will
I relent. You will be judged according to your conduct
and your actions, declares the Sovereign Lord."*

How fearful is the wrath of God. God is so displeased with the stubbornness of the heart. As seen throughout biblical history events taking place. Spiritually, we live in critical times. Praise be to God for giving every creation the vision of God's Word. God had shown the world that actions result in consequences therefore a man must stand firm, strong, and courageous in all things, even if his very own life is taken from him. Long suffering has strengthened, shaped and molded us by the grace of God.

God had opened the heart to understand that if it did not occur, none can be as it is today. The Lord does not desire for his creations to be in darkness, but to be filled with knowledge and insight of the freedom to love and honor God completely with no reservations. What great blessings it is to have the breath of life and to make a difference in the world, to see the beauty of a newborn infant through the eyes of God! Praise God for his glorious eternal love of generosity to create humanity in his own image. May the undying love of Jesus Christ be preached throughout all generations.

Works Cited

Psalm 63:1-3. The Holy Bible. NIV. 1973.

1 Chronicles 28: 9. The Holy Bible. NIV. 1973

1 John 4: 18. The Holy Bible. NIV. 1973

2 Corinthians 10: 5. The Holy Bible. NIV. 1973

Romans 15: 13. The Holy Bible. NIV. 1973

Romans 12: 2. The Holy Bible. NIV. 1973

Jeremiah 3: 15. The Holy Bible. NIV. 1973

Jeremiah 3: 22. The Holy Bible. NIV. 1973

Deuteronomy 20: 2- 4. The Holy Bible. NIV. 1973

Matthew 19: 26. The Holy Bible. NIV. 1973

Jeremiah 17: 7- 8. The Holy Bible. NIV. 1973

Hebrews 12: 2. The Holy Bible. NIV. 1973

2 Samuel 19: 6- 8. The Holy Bible. NIV. 1973

Jeremiah 17: 9. The Holy Bible. NIV. 1973

Psalm 22: 10. The Holy Bible. NIV. 1973

2 Samuel 11: 2. The Holy Bible. NIV. 1973

John 8: 7. The Holy Bible. NIV. 1973

1 Samuel 16: 7. The Holy Bible. NIV. 1973

Psalms 106:3. The Holy Bible. NIV. 1973

Genesis 45:7. The Holy Bible. NIV. 1973

Hebrews 12: 11. The Holy Bible. NIV. 1973

Romans 5: 3. The Holy Bible. NIV. 1973

Matthew 10: 28. The Holy Bible. NIV. 1973

1 John 4: 12. The Holy Bible. NIV. 1973

Romans 10:17. The Holy Bible. NIV. 1973

Acts 2: 17. The Holy Bible. NIV. 1973

Acts 19: 18. The Holy Bible. NIV. 1973

John 3: 14 – 17. The Holy Bible. NIV. 1973

John 16: 13. The Holy Bible. NIV. 1973

Luke 13: 3. The Holy Bible. NIV. 1973

Act 17: 30. The Holy Bible. NIV. 1973

Luke 12: 8. The Holy Bible. NIV. 1973

Romans 10: 9. The Holy Bible. NIV. 1973

Matthew 10: 32. The Holy Bible. NIV. 1973

Matthew 3: 13 – 17. The Holy Bible. NIV. 1973

Colossians 2: 12. The Holy Bible. NIV. 1973

Act 2: 38. The Holy Bible. NIV. 1973

1 Corinthians 1: 9. The Holy Bible. NIV. 1973

Revelations 2: 10. The Holy Bible. NIV. 1973

Deuteronomy 7: 9. The Holy Bible. NIV. 1973

1 Corinthians 15: 3. The Holy Bible. NIV. 1973

Ephesians 2: 15-18. The Holy Bible. NIV. 1973

John 16: 15. The Holy Bible. NIV. 1973

Hebrews 2: 14-18. The Holy Bible. NIV. 1973

1 Corinthians 7: 5. The Holy Bible. NIV. 1973

Jonah 4:10-11. The Holy Bible. NIV. 1973

Genesis 2: 18. The Holy Bible. NIV. 1973

Proverbs 31: 10- 12. The Holy Bible. NIV. 1973

Ephesians 5: 25 – 27. The Holy Bible. NIV. 1973

John 16: 33. The Holy Bible. NIV. 1973

Galatians 5: 22. The Holy Bible. NIV. 1973

Isaiah 56: 4-5. The Holy Bible. NIV. 1973

Deuteronomy 8: 2-5. The Holy Bible. NIV. 1973

John 4: 34. The Holy Bible. NIV. 1973

John 16:13. The Holy Bible. NIV. 1973

1 John 1: 9. The Holy Bible. NIV. 1973

Luke 12: 8. The Holy Bible. NIV. 1973

Act 17: 30. The Holy Bible. NIV. 1973

Job 22: 21. The Holy Bible. NIV. 1973

Jeremiah 17: 7 – 82. The Holy Bible. NIV. 1973

Corinthians 7: 10. The Holy Bible. NIV. 1973

Isaiah 66: 2. The Holy Bible. NIV. 1973

John 3: 3. The Holy Bible. NIV. 1973

John 16: 13. The Holy Bible. NIV. 1973

John 14: 6. The Holy Bible. NIV. 1973

Jeremiah 10: 10. The Holy Bible. NIV. 1973

Psalms 116: 1-2. The Holy Bible. NIV. 1973

Matthew 18: 10. The Holy Bible. NIV. 1973

Mark 14: 38. The Holy Bible. NIV. 1973

Genesis 3: 13. The Holy Bible. NIV. 1973

Proverbs 8: 13 – 14. The Holy Bible. NIV. 1973

Luke 22: 31 – 32. The Holy Bible. NIV. 1973

2 Corinthians 6:4-10. The Holy Bible. NIV. 1973

Romans 2: 9. The Holy Bible. NIV. 1973

Hebrews 4:12. The Holy Bible. NIV. 1973

Romans 9: 18. The Holy Bible. NIV. 1973

Jeremiah 17: 10. The Holy Bible. NIV. 1973

Jeremiah 9: 1. The Holy Bible. NIV. 1973

Jeremiah 25: 9. The Holy Bible. NIV. 1973

Jeremiah 25: 18. The Holy Bible. NIV. 1973

Jeremiah 9: 7. The Holy Bible. NIV. 1973

Jeremiah 9: 1. The Holy Bible. NIV. 1973

Jeremiah 25: 9. The Holy Bible. NIV. 1973

Jeremiah 25: 18. The Holy Bible. NIV. 1973

Jeremiah 9: 7. The Holy Bible. NIV. 1973

2 Kings 17: 13. The Holy Bible. NIV. 1973

1 King 11: 35. The Holy Bible. NIV. 1973

1 King 12: 19. The Holy Bible. NIV. 1973

2 chronicles 11:4. The Holy Bible. NIV. 1973

2 King 17: 40-41. The Holy Bible. NIV. 1973

Ezekiel 28: 14. The Holy Bible. NIV. 1973

Ezekiel 28: 17. The Holy Bible. NIV. 1973

John 17: 24. The Holy Bible. NIV. 1973

Genesis 2: 7. The Holy Bible. NIV. 1973

Philippians 3: 13 – 14. The Holy Bible. NIV. 1973

Revelation 4: 11. The Holy Bible. NIV. 1973

Ezekial 24: 14. The Holy Bible. NIV. 1973

Printed in the United States
By Bookmasters